Beauty in the Madness

Miranda Rivas

BookLeaf Publishing

Beauty in the Madness © 2023 Miranda Rivas

Presentation by *BookLeaf Publishing*

Web: www.bookleafpub.com

E-mail: info@bookleafpub.com

ISBN:9789358318340

First edition 2023

Vulnerable

Holding my feelings in, is what I do best
It comes like second nature, I must confess
Though I know it is not healthy,
But to me it is a weakness
To let someone in, to show them my uniqueness

The fear of giving too much
The fear of receiving too little
The fear of being touched
The fear of not being beneficial

Feelings are complex emotions
That are not yet mastered
Being in uncomfortable positions
Will just result in a disaster

Happy?

Are they happy with their life?
Knowing that something does not feel right
Are they happy with their job?
Knowing that they are constantly being robbed
Are they happy being single?
Knowing they hate to go out and mingle
Are they happy living alone?
Knowing they might not ever be able to call it a
home

Will they ever be truly happy?
In this world full of uncertainty.
They cannot let anyone see them imperfectly
Need to get it together, need to keep it classy
Happiness will happen
Focus on the law of attraction

Name

Mind your business
Instead of getting involved
Remember to create some distance
Watch how you will evolve
New beginnings become within reach
Demand greatness
Anticipate the breach

Breath

Relax, deep breath's

The pressure building up in the chest
Too difficult to control
Hard to breathe, the tightness seems to increase

Relax, deep breath's

The world seems to be closing in
Vision starts to blur
All there is to hear is a high pitch ring

Relax, deep breath's

Trying to be in control
But the tears start to fall
Body starts to shake
Can't stay in one place

Relax, deep breath's

Focus on what's around
Listen to the way the water flows
Feel the cool breeze on your face
Feel yourself start to regain control

Relax, deep breath's

Friends

Friendships come
Friendships go
Friendships blossom
Friendships flow

Some may drain you
While others refrain you

But be willing to remove the toxicity
To have a life with simplicity

Unhealed

I let you in
Too ignorant to see the truth
Caught up in a fantasy
Of what I thought was love
Was only a tragedy

You left me on stand by
While your plane took off
I stood there frozen, as things fell apart
Still in disbelief
How could I let myself be so naive

Others around could not see
That I was the one that wanted an out
But I did not know what that could mean
Caught up with worry of what may happen
If I was the one to set you free
What a fool for me to think that you would
choose me
Lord knows I would have been suck in misery

Hai

Only called when you needed to vent
It did not matter if you left a dent
Go on and on about how this person made you
feel
It is always the same old story, the same old reel

Not thinking for a second what I may be going
through
Try to differentiate who's, who
Fooled me, portrayed like you cared
Dimmed my light, I was not prepared

Not a friend
Only wanted a distraction, someone willing to
bend
I will be on my way, no disrespect
Next time you want to talk to me, come correct

Twin

Inseparable from the start
Could not stand to be apart
Shared many moments together
Until you left the cold weather

The memory of that day remains vivid
My heart ached like I predicted
Tears rolling down all three faces
We were about to start different phases

Understand I needed you both
Wished you could have stayed close
Felt confined, felt lost, felt cheated
I could not stay and feel completed

Reunited, words unspoken
A new path ready to begin
A bond that will never be broken
Always, my twin

Pure

All she wants is a simple life
To stay in one place
Always feeling safe

Where she can travel the world
Go through an emotional journey
Experience the wildest of fantasies
With no means of worry

Feeling the warmth of her blanket
The smell of french vanilla coffee
The heat on her skin from the crackling fire
As she is cozied up in her favorite spot
This is where she truly belongs

Fictional

The love that you seek does not seem to exist
The fictional love that every one speaks of

The kind of love where you are inseparable from
the start
The kind of love where your heart aches
whenever apart
The kind of love where your breath escapes
when your eyes meet
The kind of love where you crave their touch
Crave their smell
Crave their comfort
Crave their essences

The kind of love that cannot be explained
The kind of love that feeds your soul
When you can finally be you, with no
complaints
That is the kind of love you seek

I Wonder

Wondering what life would have been if you
were more involved
Wondering if you saw what you caused
Wondering if you share the same pain
Wondering if you hold the blame

Trying to mend what once was damaged
A life without you, I did not want to manage
Up until this day I still cannot explain
All my hurt and pain
Though you are ready for me to share
I am still hesitant, waiting for you to leave again

I.N.R

Conflicted on what words to use
There is much to say, but cannot choose
Have no intention to offend
Need to speak truth

Could not imagine life without you
Emotions start to flare with just the thought
Defensive in situations, but it comes from the
heart
Though certain aspects should have been done
different
I cannot blame you for the life you went through

One of a kind
Only one I need
Singing that song proudly
The one from my sweet sixteen

Acissej

Tossing, turning
Hoping you changed your mind
Frustrated, felt abandoned
Knowing what you left behind

Started a chain reaction
Yet did not know it
Life was beginning to change
Yet you did not quit

My role model
Powerful, fearless, independent
Painted a path not everyone can follow
Trying my best to make you proud

Blank

Something is missing
Not sure if there is a spark
Trying not to overthink

Would it be possible?
Something might be blocking these feelings
Is it on purpose?
Have these emotions been turned off?

Too much pain
Not enough joy
Feeling numb, disconnected
It was only a matter of time
Until those walls became infected

History

The past has a way of repeating itself
Until a change happens
Realize the mistakes that were made
Realize nothing good came from that place
Many will not want to take blame
Until pride is proclaimed

The ability to grow
The ability to heal
The ability to know your worth

Break Away

Behind the scenes
Reset the mind
Erase the negativity
Accept the possibilities
Knowledge is growth

Abandon the insecurities
Witness the purities
Accomplish what is in range
Yearn for change

Unseen

It will get foggy,
Vision will be obscured

Until lessons are endured

Cancerian

Compassionate,
Considerate,
Caring
Traits easily taken advantage of

Sensitive,
Sentimental,
Yet Intuitive
Traits believed to be of the wise

Protective and Loyal until the end
Calmer by the waves of the salty sea
Tread lightly, moods can be unseen

Hope

Harness inner beauty
Optimize potential to glow
Patience is a speciality
Embody strength, enjoy the show

Perspective

Take a step back
Switch the view
Instead of focusing on what is lacking
Focus on unpacking the truth

Judgement comes effortlessly
Seems almost automatic
With a switch in position
Events may be problematic

Home

Lasting memories
Irreplaceable
Tranquil energies
Transferable
Loyal for centuries
Extraordinary

Forever in the heart
Engaged from the start
Reflecting on the evolution
Remembering the seclusion
Yearning for a return

www.ingramcontent.com/pod-product-compliance
Lightning Source LLC
Chambersburg PA
CBHW071254140726
47996CB00007B/2841